I0168026

Challenge Choice Change

HOW TO BE A BETTER LEADER
IN 18 DAYS

ISBN 978-0-9575584-5-8
Pack Leader Publications

What do you want to be when you grow up?

We have all heard this question before at some stage in our life. You might have had one of the more traditional aspirations to be an astronaut, fireman, footballer, ballerina or possibly a more recent phenomenon of reality TV star or celebrity, but I guarantee you that very few (if any) of us answered that question by saying "I want to be a leader".

This is typically how it happens and our journey as a leader begins. We start our career in one field of interest or expertise and then gradually it creeps up on us until one day we find ourselves in a situation where we are responsible for leading others. Some people may consciously set out their path from an early age but in reality too many people simply drift or are promoted into positions where they are expected to lead.

What happens next? How do you become equipped with the knowledge, skills and competences to be an effective leader? The typical answer is that you get sent on a leadership development course and that's usually where the problems really begin!

Just stop for a moment and think about your own journey as a leader. Here are some initial questions to think about and help you explore how you have reached the situation you find yourself in today.

When did you officially become a leader?

. . . .

When did you actually start leading others?

. . . .

How were you prepared for your first experience as a leader?

. . . .

. . . .

How much leadership development have you already undertaken?

. . . .

What three words/phrases would you use to describe being an effective leader?

. . . .

. . . .

. . . .

Is leadership development broken?

Leadership development is big business. It is a thriving industry attracting a staggering investment from customers every year. However, research over recent years by respected global companies such as McKinsey, PWC and Deloitte, consistently suggests that one of the top challenges facing organisations across the globe is a lack of sufficient, competent and talented leaders.

With huge investments still being made in leadership development why should this be the case?

On one side there is an input called leadership development. On the other side there is the output, which should clearly be to have many more effective leaders as a result of all the development taking place.

But what is happening in reality is that there is a disconnect between the input (leadership development) and the output (developed leaders) and this gap remains an issue for far too many organisations.

Are we continuing to pour investment into something that is no longer fit for purpose? Is leadership development broken or do we need to realign our focus and investment on the output and focus on leader development instead?

Leadership development research

Leadership has always been a key topic for academic research and study and there is some excellent work being done. Unfortunately, it is often published in journals that most people don't read and is written in the language of academia, which many find difficult to understand and relate to. This is a shame because it means that the range and depth of high quality information being produced by the academic community is rarely accessible to the practitioners whose job it is to lead people every day.

The first time I had to read an academic paper, I spent more time working out what the big words meant than I did thinking about the findings and key messages. However, over the past fifteen years, I have got better, and part of my own research has been to synthesise the multitude of leadership theories and models presented by the academic community and balance them by looking at what leaders do practically in day-to-day real world applications.

This involved working with leaders across the full spectrum from public to private sector, frontline supervisors to CEOs, aspiring leaders to well established leaders, leaders working in the UK, USA, Europe and the Middle East. During this time, I have focused on identifying and researching what it is that makes some leaders so much more effective than others and what I have discovered is really quite simple!

Leadership development does NOT develop leaders!

The first thing I can tell you is that we need to be much clearer in our interpretation and more precise in our vocabulary, particularly around 'leadership' and 'leaders'.

Leadership is a process. Every organisation has processes and therefore already has leadership in place, to a greater or lesser extent. Think about all the processes you have experienced at some stage in your life - performance reviews, appraisals, team briefings, strategic planning, goal setting, recruitment, induction, coaching, mentoring – to name a few! All these processes are fundamental building blocks of any organisation's practice and are therefore part of the leadership infrastructure.

If we accept that leadership is a process then surely it follows that **leadership development** is the **development of a process.**

There is a place for this because organisations need to build knowledge, concepts and understanding in their processes but this should not be confused with the need to support and develop their people as leaders. Organisations need to do things differently if they want to build capacity within their leaders and stop focusing on developing leadership (the process) and start putting a much greater emphasis on developing the people.

This sounds so obvious but let's use a simple illustration to unpick it and reinforce the core message. Consider driving a car – this is a process – and remember that a process can be taught and a process can be learned.

Does traffic always flow smoothly and safely because everyone is a good and effective driver?

Of course not! It depends on how each individual driver behaves while implementing the process of driving. In other words, it is the person's ability to **be** a driver and their **behaviour** as a driver that counts and supports their effectiveness.

The same principle holds true with leadership. An organisation can have all the leadership processes in place but it is how people behave when implementing these processes that distinguishes their ability to be effective and have an impact as a leader.

So how does an effective leader behave?

The Effective Leader Inventory (ELi) is a construct that has distilled decades of research into a single framework. It identifies 18 behavioural elements that are critical to the effectiveness of a leader and indicates the four factors that exert an influence.

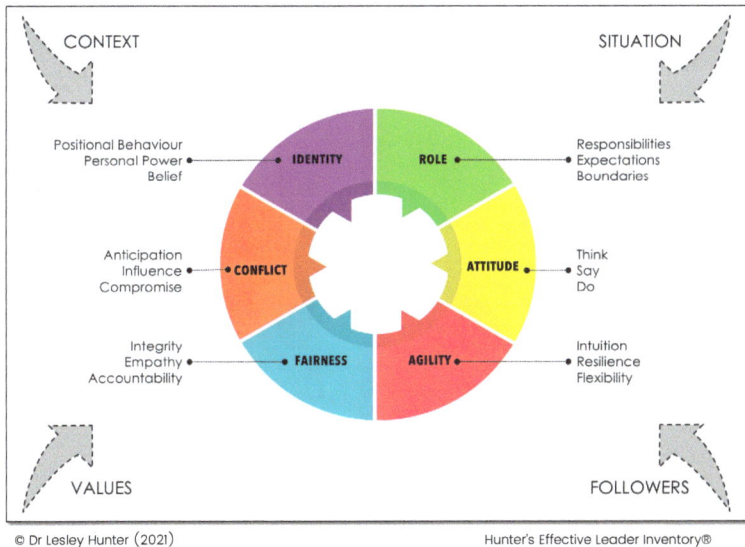

CONTEXT

SITUATION

Positional Behaviour
Personal Power
Belief

IDENTITY

ROLE

Responsibilities
Expectations
Boundaries

Anticipation
Influence
Compromise

CONFLICT

ATTITUDE

Think
Say
Do

Integrity
Empathy
Accountability

FAIRNESS

AGILITY

Intuition
Resilience
Flexibility

VALUES

FOLLOWERS

© Dr Lesley Hunter (2021)   Hunter's Effective Leader Inventory®

It is the combination of these 18 behaviours that determine a leader's behaviour at any given point in time.

Identity

This dimension focuses on an individual's internal awareness and representation of what it means to be a leader.

The elements in Identity are:

- Positional Behaviour
- Personal Power
- Belief

Positional Behaviour is focused on an individual's own perception and identity as a leader, and their subsequent ability to motivate, influence and guide others' actions. It is not about their status, job title or the degree of authority they are perceived to exert in an organisational hierarchy or structure.

Personal Power is focused on an individual's ability to recognise and accept their internal state of mind leading to the capacity to exert power on their own emotions and actions. It is not about holding power over another person or influencing or manipulating externally.

Belief is focused on an individual's internal perspective and core view of themself as a leader. It is a state of mind that feeds into their Identity.

Role

This dimension considers the parameters within which the individual is operating as a leader.

The elements in Role are:

- Responsibilities
- Expectations
- Boundaries

Responsibilities is related to an individual's understanding of the purpose, function and roles of both themself (as a leader) and their team, along with the tasks and contribution expected from each team member.

Expectations is focused on an individual's understanding of the expectations associated with different roles; their own (as a leader) and also the individuals within their team. Expectations can be defined in terms of behaviour, targets, objectives and outcomes, and can therefore be measured as performance in these areas.

Boundaries is focused on an individual's understanding of the boundaries of different roles; their own (as a leader) and also the individuals within their team. Boundaries need to be defined in relation to tasks, leading and developing others, as well as the emotional boundaries the individual will experience as a leader.

Attitude

This dimension refers to the external manifestation of the behaviour associated with the individual's identity and role as a leader.

The elements in Attitude are:

- Think
- Say
- Do

Think is the cognitive element of attitude. It relates to an individual's thought processes and decision-making strategies, including the use of visualisation, creative thinking and mental agility. The most effective leaders are self-aware and consequently understand how their thinking processes affect their behaviour and performance.

Say is the communicative element of attitude. It relates to the way an individual communicates their thoughts and feelings and takes account of the tone, style, consistency and clarity of their approach (verbally and non-verbally).

Do is the action-oriented element of attitude by turning an individual's thoughts and feelings into action. A leader is often judged by their actions, i.e. what they do and how they do it.

Agility

This dimension focuses on how an individual broadens their behavioural repertoire and ensures that, as a leader, they are agile enough to handle different situations and interactions with different individuals, including the balance between their conscious and unconscious decision-making process.

The elements in Agility are:

- Intuition
- Resilience
- Flexibility

Intuition is focused on an individual's ability to recognise patterns, understand their own strengths and weaknesses and be able to balance logic and intuitive decision-making. .

Resilience is focused on an individual's ability to learn from experiences, including mistakes, and to handle stressful and difficult situations. It links to how they manage and regulate their own emotional state in order to maintain their personal and professional well-being.

Flexibility is focused on an individual's ability to handle uncertainty and ambiguity. It is about having strategies to cope and adapt in unfamiliar situations and being able to handle and embrace change.

Fairness

This dimension considers the way an individual behaves during interactions with others.

The elements in Fairness are:

- Integrity
- Empathy
- Accountability

Integrity is strongly rooted in values and is focused on the way in which an individual treats people. It is associated with dignity, respect, honesty, visibility and developing trust.

Empathy is focused on how an individual develops relationships and shared understanding with others. It is also about the development of psychological contracts with followers. Empathy is the ability to identify and understand another's situation, feelings and motives. It is often described as putting yourself in the other person's shoes or seeing things through someone else's eyes.

Accountability is about an individual holding themself, and others, responsible (to account) for the commitments they are expected to fulfil. It is focused on the individual understanding the impact of their actions as a leader and taking responsibility for the outcomes but is also about holding others accountable for their contribution as followers.

Conflict

This dimension refers to an individual's behaviour in relation to interacting and engaging with others to achieve a specified outcome.

The elements in Conflict are:

- Anticipation
- Influence
- Compromise

Anticipation is the forward-thinking element of the conflict dimension. It is focused on scanning, assessing and being alert to changing conditions and potential opportunities for conflict. It is also about developing strategies to recognise situations and support decision-making.

Influence is the capacity to change or affect someone or something and is focused on building networks, communities and alliances to reach collaborative decisions and outcomes.

Compromise is focused on the ability to see others' points of view and take appropriate action to achieve required outcomes. It also considers an individual's capacity to handle different forms of conflict (task, inter-personal, emotional) and to resolve disputes.

Introducing Challenge Choice Change

Now that we have a clear framework for leader behaviour, it is time to switch the focus from leadership development and consider a new approach to **leader development.**

Challenge Choice Change (CCC) is a triple-loop coaching model that evolved from research into authentic leadership and the stages of development an individual needs to go through from self-awareness (challenge) and self-regulation (choice) to developing authentic self-leader behaviours (change).

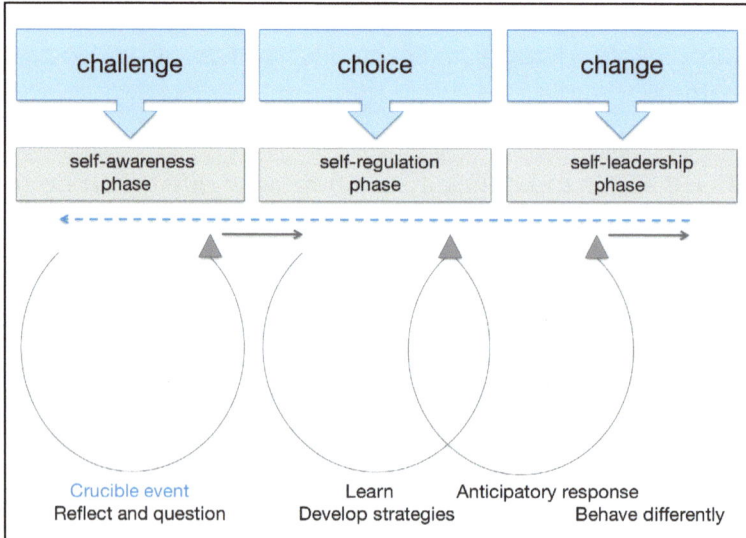

challenge	choice	change
self-awareness phase	self-regulation phase	self-leadership phase

Crucible event   Learn   Anticipatory response
Reflect and question   Develop strategies   Behave differently

Challenge Choice Change (CCC) Model © Dr Lesley Hunter

Consider this as a fitness campaign for developing leaders. This book will use the CCC model in a reflective journal format to kick start your fitness campaign by working three different groups of muscles to develop your effectiveness as a leader over the next 18 days.

- Challenge muscles (self-awareness)
- Choice muscles (self-regulation)
- Change muscles (self-lead)

As you work through each of these groups of muscles, you are engaging a different aspect of leader effectiveness. As with any fitness regime, there are some basic rules and principles if you want to get the best from your experience.

1. It has to be part of your daily routine and ongoing practice.
2. You need to challenge your existing mindset.
3. You need a baseline of where you are at the start and a clear understanding of what you are trying to achieve.
4. You need to change your habits. You may have to replace some of them with new different behaviour.
5. You have to work at it and be prepared to go through the pain.
6. You need to acknowledge and celebrate your successes and build on your achievements.
7. Accept it won't happen overnight – take small incremental steps.

Work your **challenge** muscles

These muscles are there to develop an identity, a mindset and raise your self-awareness as a leader. They are worked by firstly forming a clear identity of what it means to be a leader and then using this as your reference to keep checking through continuous self-reflection.

To establish your identity, you need to create an internal awareness and representation of what it actually means to be a leader. You should not rely on status, job title or position in an organisation to bestow this on you but should define your identity as a leader by how you believe a leader should behave.

By working your challenge muscles, you will learn to accept that you have the power, motivation and belief to be a leader. You will begin to understand how your behaviour might be perceived and the impact it can have on others, which will help you to anticipate how your followers will respond and be clear about the outcomes you are likely to get.

By flexing your challenge muscles you will know how you measure up to your own internal identity as a leader. You will also start recognising your own strengths to maintain and have the clarity to know precisely what behaviour needs to be the focus for your future development as a leader.

Work your **choice** muscles

These muscles are there to help you build flexibility in your behaviour. They are worked through exercising self-regulation where you make a conscious decision about how you will behave in any given situation.

The difficulty is how do you self-regulate if you don't know the range of behaviours available for you to select and choose from? So these are the muscles you really need to work on and keep developing – this is the heavy lifting aspect of learning to be a leader where you need to learn different techniques and strategies to increase your behavioural flexibility in different situations.

Work your **change** muscles

These muscles are there to help you self-lead. It is all very well having a clear identity and wide range of behavioural choice available but if you don't take action then you are not going to have any impact as a leader.

By working your change muscles, you take responsibility for leading yourself and align your identity with your behaviour. Exercising these muscles is about turning up and owning the actions you take.

Now think back to the research that is highlighting the challenge for many organisations to recruit and retain effective leaders. My interpretation is that there is a widening gap caused by throwing investment in leadership development at people who did not have an identity, a mindset or a fitness regime to develop them as leaders in the first place.

How to use this book

Using the Effective Leader Inventory (ELi) as the core framework, this book will take you through an 18-day personal development programme with a different element as the focus for each of the days. You will be prompted to flex your Challenge Choice Change (CCC) muscles and to record your learning in a journal.

- For 18 days, read the relevant **challenge** statements associated with the element for that day.

- Select the statement that is having the biggest impact on your performance as a leader right now. This may be a negative impact where you need to do something differently or could be a positive impact where you need to consciously focus on doing more of something that is currently working well.

- Make a **choice** and identify **one thing** you can do for a day that will improve your performance against this statement. It is really important to keep the activity simple, realistic and manageable.

- Keep your focus on that activity throughout the day. Don't try and be too ambitious. You are aiming to disrupt your current pattern of behaviour and individual small incremental steps will build into accelerated progress over the period of your 18-day programme.

- Each evening, record your thoughts and experiences in the daily journal. Please do not skip this step because this is where you will be able to reflect and identify your key learning.

At the end of the 18 days, take some time to read your daily journal entries and reflect on the **changes** you have made. Remember that you must hold yourself to account and be honest with yourself.

The 18-day programme will kick-start your development but to change, integrate and embed different patterns of behaviour will take time - remember it will not happen overnight.

Before you start . . .

It is very easy to start something with the best intentions but the most difficult part of any development programme is maintaining motivation and seeing it through to completion. It is inevitable that your focus will waiver at some stage during the 18 days. When it does, come back to this section and pick an affirmation that will motivate you to continue.

Get a grip!   I am learning something
                     new every day

                                    Slowly but surely
                                    one day at a time

I can do this – I will do this – I am doing this

Now add some of your own affirmations that will inspire and support you for the next 18 days.

. . . .

. . . .

01

Identity

Positional Behaviour

Positional Behaviour is focused on your own perception and identity as a leader and your subsequent ability to motivate, influence and guide others' actions.

It is not about your status, job title or the degree of authority you are perceived to exert due to your position in an organisational hierarchy or structure.

Challenge

Which of these statements is having the biggest impact on your performance as a leader right now and how is it working for you?

    A. I have a clear frame of reference for my position as a leader.

    B. I have a clear understanding of how to behave as a leader.

    C. I create strong psychological contracts with my followers.

Choice

Making a conscious choice, what **one thing** will you do differently **today**?

Change

Reflecting on what you have learned, what will you take forward and integrate into your behaviour to improve your performance as a leader?

. . . .

. . . .

. . . .

. . . .

. . . .

. . . .

. . . .

. . . .

. . . .

. . . .

Day 01 – Identity – Positional Behaviour

02

Identity

Personal Power

Personal Power is focused on your ability to recognise and accept your internal state of mind leading to the capacity to exert power on your own emotions and actions. It is not about holding power over another person or influencing or manipulating externally.

Challenge

Which of these statements is having the biggest impact on your performance as a leader right now and how is it working for you?

A. I have the personal power to motivate myself.

B. I can control and influence the outcomes of my decisions and actions.

C. I have the personal power to choose how I feel and respond in any given situation.

Choice

Making a conscious choice, what **one thing** will you do differently **today**?

Change

Reflecting on what you have learned, what will you take forward and integrate into your behaviour to improve your performance as a leader?

. . . .

. . . .

. . . .

. . . .

. . . .

. . . .

. . . .

. . . .

. . . .

Day 02 – Identity – Personal Power

03

Identity

Belief

Belief is focused on your internal perspective and core view of yourself as the leader – it is a state of mind that feeds into your identity.

Challenge

Which of these statements is having the biggest impact on your performance as a leader right now and how is it working for you?

    A. I believe in myself and *see* myself as a leader.

    B. I believe in what I am trying to achieve.

    C. I have confidence in my abilities as a leader.

Choice

Making a conscious choice, what **one thing** will you do differently **today**?

Change

Reflecting on what you have learned, what will you take forward and integrate into your behaviour to improve your performance as a leader?

....

....

....

....

....

....

....

....

....

Day 03 – Identity – Belief

04

Role

Responsibilities

Responsibilities is focused on your understanding of the purpose, function and roles of your team along with the tasks and contribution expected from each team member.

Challenge

Which of these statements is having the biggest impact on your performance as a leader right now and how is it working for you?

A. I understand the tasks that are required to achieve the outcome I want.

B. I understand the role of my team in relation to the organisation as a whole.

C. I can articulate the responsibilities of each individual member of my team.

Choice

Making a conscious choice, what **one thing** will you do differently **today**?

Change

Reflecting on what you have learned, what will you take forward and integrate into your behaviour to improve your performance as a leader?

. . . .

. . . .

. . . .

. . . .

. . . .

. . . .

. . . .

. . . .

. . . .

05

Role

Expectations

Expectations is focused on your understanding of what is expected associated with different roles – your own as a leader and also the individuals within your team.

Expectations can be defined in terms of behaviour, targets, objectives and outcomes, and can therefore be measured as performance in these areas.

Challenge

Which of these statements is having the biggest impact on your performance as a leader right now and how is it working for you?

A. I can define and articulate my expectations of each individual member of my team.

B. My expectations are clearly defined as targets and/or objectives.

C. I measure the performance of others in relation to the expectations of their role.

Choice

Making a conscious choice, what **one thing** will you do differently **today**?

Change

Reflecting on what you have learned, what will you take forward and integrate into your behaviour to improve your performance as a leader?

. . . .

. . . .

. . . .

. . . .

. . . .

. . . .

. . . .

. . . .

. . . .

06
Role

Boundaries

Boundaries is focused on your understanding of the boundaries of different roles – your own as the leader and also the individuals within your team.

Boundaries need to be defined in relation to tasks, leading and developing others, as well as the emotional boundaries you will experience as a leader.

Challenge

Which of these statements is having the biggest impact on your performance as a leader right now and how is it working for you?

    A.   I understand the boundaries of my own role as a leader.

    B.   I can clearly define the boundaries of each individual's role within my team.

    C.   I accept that my boundaries are not barriers or restrictions that prevent me contributing as a leader.

Choice

Making a conscious choice, what **one thing** will you do differently **today**?

Change

Reflecting on what you have learned, what will you take forward and integrate into your behaviour to improve your performance as a leader?

. . . .

. . . .

. . . .

. . . .

. . . .

. . . .

. . . .

. . . .

. . . .

Day 06 – Role – Boundaries

07
Attitude

Think

Think relates to your thought processes and decision-making strategies, including the use of visualisation, creative thinking and mental agility.

The most effective leaders are self-aware and consequently understand how they're thinking processes affect their behaviour and performance.

Challenge

Which of these statements is having the biggest impact on your performance as a leader right now and how is it working for you?

A. I think creatively when faced with unfamiliar challenges and situations.

B. I use visualisation to create a mental image and *see* what I am trying to achieve.

C. I recognise the importance of understanding *why* when making decisions and taking action.

Choice

Making a conscious choice, what **one thing** will you do differently **today**?

Change

Reflecting on what you have learned, what will you take forward and integrate into your behaviour to improve your performance as a leader?

. . . .

. . . .

. . . .

. . . .

. . . .

. . . .

. . . .

. . . .

. . . .

Day 07 – Attitude - Think

08
Attitude

Say

Say relates to the way you communicate your thoughts and feelings and takes account of the tone, style, consistency and clarity of your approach (verbally and non-verbally).

Challenge

Which of these statements is having the biggest impact on your performance as a leader right now and how is it working for you?

A. I communicate my thoughts clearly and concisely.

B. I recognise and use a range of delivery styles to ensure my approach is appropriate for the audience.

C. I say what I mean and mean what I say.

Choice

Making a conscious choice, what **one thing** will you do differently **today**?

Change

Reflecting on what you have learned, what will you take forward and integrate into your behaviour to improve your performance as a leader?

....

....

....

....

....

....

....

....

....

....

09
Attitude

Do

Do is the action-oriented element of attitude. A leader is often judged by their actions, i.e. what they do and how they do it.

Challenge

Which of these statements is having the biggest impact on your performance as a leader right now and how is it working for you?

A. I behave in a fair and consistent manner.

B. I create space for innovation and creativity to happen.

C. I am comfortable using emotional displays to increase my effectiveness as a leader.

Choice

Making a conscious choice, what **one thing** will you do differently **today**?

Change

Reflecting on what you have learned, what will you take forward and integrate into your behaviour to improve your performance as a leader?

. . . .

. . . .

. . . .

. . . .

. . . .

. . . .

. . . .

. . . .

. . . .

10

Agility

Intuition

Intuition is focused on your ability to recognise patterns, understand your strengths and weaknesses and be able to balance logic and intuitive decision-making.

Effective leaders can distinguish between instinct, which is a hardwired autonomous reflex action, and intuition (i.e. feeling of knowing or tip of the tongue phenomenon).

Challenge

Which of these statements is having the biggest impact on your performance as a leader right now and how is it working for you?

A. I balance an intuitive approach with logical argument.

B. I know when something is right.

C. I recognise patterns linked to my intuitive decision-making.

Choice

Making a conscious choice, what **one thing** will you do differently **today**?

Change

Reflecting on what you have learned, what will you take forward and integrate into your behaviour to improve your performance as a leader?

. . . .

. . . .

. . . .

. . . .

. . . .

. . . .

. . . .

. . . .

. . . .

Day 10 – Agility - Intuition

11

Agility

Resilience

Resilience is focused on your ability to learn from experiences, including mistakes, and to handle stressful and difficult situations. It links to how you manage and regulate your own emotional state in order to maintain your personal and professional well-being.

Challenge

Which of these statements is having the biggest impact on your performance as a leader right now and how is it working for you?

A. I am not afraid of experiencing failure.

B. I bounce back from disappointment by reframing the situation and using it as a learning opportunity.

C. I manage my own emotional state effectively.

Choice

Making a conscious choice, what **one thing** will you do differently **today**?

Change

Reflecting on what you have learned, what will you take forward and integrate into your behaviour to improve your performance as a leader?

. . . .

. . . .

. . . .

. . . .

. . . .

. . . .

. . . .

. . . .

. . . .

Day 11 – Agility - Resilience

12

Agility

Flexibility

Flexibility is focused on your ability to handle uncertainty and ambiguity. It is about having strategies to cope and adapt in unfamiliar situations and being able to handle and embrace change.

Leaders need to demonstrate flexibility at various levels – cognitive, behavioural and emotional.

Challenge

Which of these statements is having the biggest impact on your performance as a leader right now and how is it working for you?

A. I have developed appropriate strategies to handle uncertainty and ambiguity.

B. I embrace change.

C. I am prepared to seek out innovative and new solutions.

Choice

Making a conscious choice, what **one thing** will you do differently **today**?

Change

Reflecting on what you have learned, what will you take forward and integrate into your behaviour to improve your performance as a leader?

. . . .

. . . .

. . . .

. . . .

. . . .

. . . .

. . . .

. . . .

. . . .

. . . .

Day 12 – Agility - Flexibility

13

Fairness

Integrity

Integrity is focused on the way in which you treat people. It is associated with dignity, respect, honesty, visibility and developing trust. Integrity is an essential ingredient for a leader to be effective.

Challenge

Which of these statements is having the biggest impact on your performance as a leader right now and how is it working for you?

A. I behave in an open and transparent manner.

B. I have a strong moral code that underpins my behaviour as a leader.

C. My actions are consistent with both my personal values and the organisational values.

Choice

Making a conscious choice, what **one thing** will you do differently **today**?

Change

Reflecting on what you have learned, what will you take forward and integrate into your behaviour to improve your performance as a leader?

. . . .

. . . .

. . . .

. . . .

. . . .

. . . .

. . . .

. . . .

. . . .

Day 13 – Fairness - Integrity

14

Fairness

Empathy

Empathy is focused on how you develop relationships and shared understanding with others. It is also about the development of psychological contracts with your followers.

Challenge

Which of these statements is having the biggest impact on your performance as a leader right now and how is it working for you?

A. I build meaningful and appropriate relationships with my followers.

B. I do not confuse empathy with sympathy.

C. I have a good understanding of the impact I have on others.

Choice

Making a conscious choice, what **one thing** will you do differently **today**?

Change

Reflecting on what you have learned, what will you take forward and integrate into your behaviour to improve your performance as a leader?

. . . .

. . . .

. . . .

. . . .

. . . .

. . . .

. . . .

. . . .

. . . .

15

Fairness

Accountability

Accountability is about holding yourself, and others, "to account" for the commitments you are expected to fulfil. It is focused on understanding the impact of your actions as a leader and taking responsibility for the outcomes but is also about holding others accountable for their contribution as followers.

Challenge

Which of these statements is having the biggest impact on your performance as a leader right now and how is it working for you?

A. I regularly reflect on my own performance and hold myself accountable for the outcomes.

B. I accept credit and recognition for my successes.

C. I understand the impact of my actions.

Choice

Making a conscious choice, what **one thing** will you do differently **today**?

Change

Reflecting on what you have learned, what will you take forward and integrate into your behaviour to improve your performance as a leader?

. . . .

. . . .

. . . .

. . . .

. . . .

. . . .

. . . .

. . . .

. . . .

Day 15 – Fairness - Accountability

16

Conflict

Anticipation

Anticipation is focused on scanning, assessing and being alert to changing conditions and potential opportunities for conflict. It is also about developing strategies to recognise situations and support decision-making.

Challenge

Which of these statements is having the biggest impact on your performance as a leader right now and how is it working for you?

A. I am alert to factors and issues that could influence or de-stabilise my team.

B. I can detect emerging conflict in its earliest stages.

C. I recognise the signs and symptoms when conflict could arise.

Choice

Making a conscious choice, what **one thing** will you do differently **today**?

Change

Reflecting on what you have learned, what will you take forward and integrate into your behaviour to improve your performance as a leader?

. . . .

. . . .

. . . .

. . . .

. . . .

. . . .

. . . .

. . . .

. . . .

. . . .

17

Conflict

Influence

Influence is the capacity to change or affect someone or something and is focused on building networks, communities and alliances to reach collaborative decisions and outcomes.

Effective leaders are influence agents who use a range of tactics to influence different targets, depending on the situation at the time.

Challenge

Which of these statements is having the biggest impact on your performance as a leader right now and how is it working for you?

A. I can influence others to reach collaborative decisions and outcomes.

B. I can influence opinionated people.

C. I have a clear understanding of the difference between influence and persuasion.

Choice

Making a conscious choice, what **one thing** will you do differently **today**?

Change

Reflecting on what you have learned, what will you take forward and integrate into your behaviour to improve your performance as a leader?

. . . .

. . . .

. . . .

. . . .

. . . .

. . . .

. . . .

. . . .

. . . .

. . . .

Day 17 – Conflict - Influence

18

Conflict

Compromise

Compromise is focused on your ability to see others' points of view and take appropriate action to achieve required outcomes. It also considers your capacity to handle different forms of conflict (task, inter-personal, emotional) and to resolve disputes.

Challenge

Which of these statements is having the biggest impact on your performance as a leader right now and how is it working for you?

A. I know when it would be appropriate to compromise and when this would not be the right course of action.

B. I can resolve disputes within my team.

C. I stimulate and manage productive conflict.

Choice

Making a conscious choice, what **one thing** will you do differently **today**?

Change

Reflecting on what you have learned, what will you take forward and integrate into your behaviour to improve your performance as a leader?

. . . .

. . . .

. . . .

. . . .

. . . .

. . . .

. . . .

. . . .

. . . .

Next steps

Now that you have started your leader development fitness regime, you need to decide how to continue building and flexing your muscles.

One option is to revisit the daily statements and start the journaling process again, but this time select a different statement from each of the 18 behavioural elements. This way you will start to add additional layers to your development in each element and consolidate your behavioural change. Another approach is to focus specifically on each of the statements in one individual element or dimension if you identify an area in need of attention. The table on the next page will help you to keep a record of the statements you have used in each dimension and element to support your CCC development journey. Use the blank pages at the back of this book to summarise the key learning from your daily reflections and journals.

A key feature of the challenge stage (self-awareness) is asking for feedback from others on how they perceive your behaviour and the impact this has on the outcomes to be achieved. Although this can be daunting at first, it is often the most important step a leader can take to begin opening communication and discussion around behaviour in the workplace.

DIMENSION	ELEMENT	STATEMENT		
		A	B	C
IDENTITY	Positional Behaviour			
	Personal Power			
	Belief			
ROLE	Responsibilities			
	Expectations			
	Boundaries			
ATTITUDE	Think			
	Say			
	Do			
AGILITY	Intuition			
	Resilience			
	Flexibility			
FAIRNESS	Integrity			
	Empathy			
	Accountability			
CONFLICT	Anticipation			
	Influence			
	Compromise			

Notes

. . . .

. . . .

. . . .

School Leader Inventory (SLi)

For leaders working in educational settings, the ELi model has been adapted to create the School Leader Inventory (SLi) where the behaviours are specifically aligned with the leadership processes of self-evaluation and school improvement.

The SLi is a sophisticated self-perception instrument that considers the balance of a leader's behaviour and how this contributes to both their performance and well-being. It supports an individual's self-awareness but also benchmarks against a database of scores from other school leaders to produce a three-stage action plan and promote leader development.

To achieve this, the SLi is supported by a suite of resources, including:

- a unique online diagnostic;
- personalised profile reports;
- a toolkit of behavioural change techniques aligned to each of the 18 behavioural elements;
- an online membership program.

Visit www.school-leader-inventory.com to find out more and take advantage of the free resources and tools available.

About Lesley Hunter

Lesley has achieved a rare balance of practical experience and academic credibility for her work with leaders. Her early career in education laid the foundation for a "no nonsense" down to earth style of delivery and her ability to analyse and forensically target areas for improvement through extensive experience as a lead inspector of schools in the UK. Her work in education has transcended international and sector boundaries, from working with school principals and senior leaders in UK, Europe and throughout the Middle East to delivering leader development and innovation modules on MBA and MSc programmes for universities in the UK, Hong Kong, Singapore, United Arab Emirates and Geneva.

Lesley has a strong pedigree outside education and has worked in a consultancy capacity with senior leaders in public, private and government organisations. She has an unrivalled depth of knowledge and experience in understanding what makes leaders effective and how they can impact on the performance of any organisation.

www.lesleyhunter.com

mail@lesleyhunter.com

www.ingramcontent.com/pod-product-compliance
Lightning Source LLC
Chambersburg PA
CBHW041529090426
42738CB00035B/9